FORE THE MIND

THE MENTAL PROGRAM FOR GOLF

TROY BASSHAM

All rights reserved. No part of this book may be reproduced or transmitted in any form or by means now known or any means yet to be invented, electronic, or mechanical, including photocopying, recording, or by any information storage or retrieval system without written permission from the author or publisher, except brief inclusion of quotations in a review.

Copyright © 2015 by Mental Management® Systems LLC
and Troy Bassham. All rights reserved.

The term Mental Management® is registered
and owned by Lanny Bassham.

All rights reserved.
ISBN 978-1-934324-34-9
Printed in the United States of America

Order from
Mental Management® Systems
www.mentalmanagement.com
ph. 972-899-9640

Contents

Introduction	*i*
Foreword	*v*
Chapter 1 - Kevin	*1*
Chapter 2 - The Book	*7*
Chapter 3 - The Mental Checklist	*13*
Chapter 4 - Commitment	*21*
Chapter 5 - Preload for Putting	*29*
Chapter 6 - The Mental Program	*37*
Chapter 7 - The Point of Initiation	*43*
Chapter 8 - The Point of Alignment	*49*
Chapter 9 - The Point of Focus	*57*
Chapter 10 - The Invitational	*67*
Chapter 11 - The Classic	*77*
About the Author	*88*

Dedication

To my wife, Frances, my reason for reaching success.

To Christ, who gives me strength and makes all things possible.

To my daughters, Tori and Sydney, for making me feel like a winner each and every day.

To my father, Lanny Bassham, for developing the Mental Management® System and teaching me how to use it.

To my mother, Helen Bassham, for giving me the opportunity to teach at Mental Management Systems.

To my brother, Brian, for the support and competition growing up.

To my sister, Heather, for the encouragement you give every day.

To all my students who strive to be the best.

Introduction

Ask yourself this question, "What Percentage of my golf game is mental?" Is it 50%, 70%, or maybe 90% of the game? This is a question I ask all my clients. It doesn't matter if the player is twelve years old, playing in high school, college, or striving to be the best senior amateur in the country. It doesn't matter if the player is on the PGA tour. I ask this question to every player. The interesting part is the answer to the question.

What was your answer? Did you give it a high number? Did you give it a low number? If you gave it a low number, put this book down. It's not for you. But if you gave it 50% or higher this book may just be the answer to playing better golf. The answer to this question is interesting because it is virtually the same for a junior player all the way up to the PGA Tour professional.

When I asked Fred Funk, Jerry Kelly, Ben Crane, Justin Leonard, Rory Sabatini, and many other PGA Tour players this question the answer was the same. It's 90 to 95 percent of the game; everyone at this level can hit the shots. It's what goes on between the ears, that's the difference.

When I ask young players to amateur players this question the reply is 80% or higher. This is interesting to me because it verifies that the mental game is important at all levels of ability and all ages. Players acknowledge that not only is there a mental component but the mental component is as important, or more important, than the technical component. This requires me to ask a follow up question, "What percentage of time do you give to the mental game?"

Think about the answer you gave. If you think the mental game is 80% of the game of golf, do you give 80% of your time, money, effort and energy to the mental game? I am guessing you are thinking, "No, I don't." Why? Because I have yet to meet a player, at any level, who gives a higher number to the mental game, and actually gives close to that number to their technique. In fact, I get the opposite. If the player says the game is 80% mental, and I ask them the follow up question the reply is, "I hardly give any time, money, effort, or energy to it."

This is a problem. How can players expect to reach their true potential in the game if they almost ignore one of the critical parts to playing great golf: the control of the mental game during the round. I understand why players do this. Most books on the mental game, and there are some good ones, tell you what to do but fail to tell you how to do it. This area is the focus of my work as a performance coach. This book will guide you in implementing a strong mental system to improve consistency in your golf game. Think about it. How can you be technically consistent if you are not mentally consistent? The story you are about to read will not only tell you what you should do, but also how you can do it.

I wanted to create a book that allows readers the ability to put themselves in the position of the main character and incorporate the same techniques into their games. This book is

Introduction

told as a story, providing specific steps taken from the Mental Management® System that my father, Lanny Bassham, created. This proprietary system has helped thousands of players reach important goals and personal bests in competition.

I wasn't interested in just providing a good story to the reader. I want readers to walk away with a mental system of their own. After reading this story you will be able to create your own mental system that will give you an edge over your competition. A mental system is a defined thought process that is used during critical moments in golf. Everyone has a pre-shot routine but few can define what they are thinking about during the shot routine. After implementing these Mental Management® techniques to your golf game you will have a detailed and defined mental system that will allow you to play better golf on a consistent basis.

Increasingly, there are two kinds of players: those who have a mental system and those who don't. After reading this book you will find yourself in the first category.

Troy Bassham
Dallas, Texas

FOREWORD

Shawn Humphries

I met the Bassham Team through a friend (David Andres) a few years ago. His son Grant was a student in my year-round youth academy. David mentioned that Lanny and Troy had an amazing mental training system called Mental Management®. Lanny and Troy personally used this system to perform at the highest levels in sport performance by winning a Gold and Silver medal in the Olympics, as well as setting multiple national and world records.

Let's get something straight; there are plenty of sports psychologists out there in the market place. I have personally talked with, listened to, and interviewed some of the best. Being a Golf Magazine Top 100 Teacher In America, I have access to some of the best resources in the world. You see, I've been teaching, coaching, and training golf for over a quarter century. And in my lifetime, I've never met a sports psychologist who has personally won a major event using the method he teaches to his clients. And to me the highest level is Olympic competition. It's the grandest scale by which to be measured when it comes to world competition.

So what's missing with the current psychologist? I have

yet to find one that can define his program and call it a system. Systems are defined! I would never teach, or train, a student learning the golf swing without defining what, why, where, and when it needs to be done. I always walk them through the steps. If you don't have a systematic way of doing it, how can you communicate it to your students. How are you going to teach them the language of your system?

We can all agree we want more consistency in our golf games, right? In order to have consistency you must be able to duplicate something on a regular basis and have some sense of mastery. The only way you can master something is you MUST have a system in place.

Systems provide defined check points, allowing you to identify and implement immediate solutions to your game for consistent and repeatable results.

A mental system is critical to performing at your best. Imagine if you could remove yourself from the competitive environment on demand, very much like playing a practice round of golf. Imagine if you had a system that allowed you to commit to every shot on the golf course. More importantly, the system allowed you to respond to every situation you encountered, like our first responders do when we have a national disaster. They are trained to respond to the situation, not react. This system trains you to respond.

We are currently the only golf academy in the world that is fully certified to use the Mental Management® System, and Troy Bassham (Master Coach) is our director of Mental Management®. In the first year we rolled out the curriculum, 80% of our youth academy members achieved their 12 month goals in 5 months. This system is a game changer. More importantly, it weaves right into the landscape of the academy and is what we truly pride ourselves on.

With this book Troy has taken the Mental Management®

System his father, Lanny Bassham, created and put it into an incredible story form that truly resonates. *Fore the Mind* is an incredible read and I know you will thoroughly enjoy his writing. Read, learn, and implement these lessons, and you will have more success on and off the golf course than you have ever had in your life! I know—our academy is living proof.

Shawn Humphries is Director and Owner of Shawn Humphries Golf Performance (Youth Academy) at Grapevine Municipal Golf Course in Grapevine, TX, a golf performance-training academy that specializes in developing youth golfers into world class performers. His performance training has produced over 1,500 individual champions. They range from Junior World, AJGA, NCAA, Canadian, Web.com, LPGA, and European Tour winners.

Chapter 1

Kevin

Kevin held his head slightly turned to the left, toward the spectators. His eyes were piercing through the audience as if they were not there. His lips pressed together as though he was about to blurt something out. It was like he was in another world while everyone else was watching his every move. Approaching his third shot on the easy par four, Kevin shook his head saying to himself "No! No! No!"

At 105 yards out, he is desperately needing to save par to stay in contention. The pressure is mounting as the holes get fewer and fewer and the crowds get larger and larger. It is apparent that he knows where he stands. Once in the lead by two shots, Kevin is now one shot back with only four holes left.

You can imagine the thoughts that must be going through his mind as he pulls out a wedge and gets ready to hit the shot. He takes two practice swings before he takes a deep breath and steps into the shot. One look to the target, he settles his feet and takes a second quick look. As his head comes back to the ball, the club immediately moves back in his takeaway. The shot is off line to the right but sticks pin high about 25 feet from the hole.

It is a painful place to be. He has been performing well but one bad hole is leading to another. "If only I could keep things going and par the way out," turns to "I have to birdie two out of the next three!" These are the thoughts that are going on in Kevin's mind. Now, as he approaches the green, he is thinking "I have to make this putt." Outcome and results consume his conscious mind. I have seen this look many times on Kevin's face.

As luck would have it, he two putts for bogey. He is now two shots back and only has three holes left. This is not uncommon for him, nor for other players. It is hard to keep playing your best under pressure. It is even harder when you have not played well in a long time. That is exactly where Kevin stands.

It has been more than a year since he has been in position to win a tournament. He has won at every level of competition except the tour level. He has struggled to stay on the tour, and now he struggles to finish strong in this tournament. As the final three holes are played out, Kevin falls short of a comeback. He manages to par out the final three holes and finishes in fifth place. Hardly the finish he was expecting at the beginning of the final round, but such is golf.

I have followed Kevin's career from day one. Like many uncles who do not have kids of their own, I took a liking to Kevin from the day he was born. His father, James, and I were not only brothers, we were close friends who pushed each other to play our best in this great sport.

James was a great player who won at every level. As a junior player, he carried himself beyond his years. He was the kid who could walk with confidence without coming across as cocky or arrogant. He could hit shots that amazed his competition. Other players would look at him and just shake their heads. He was a top recruit and only got better in college.

He held the school record for the lowest round and won more tournaments than anyone in school history. He was extremely talented and loved to win. He made it a point to goal set for each tournament, both as an individual as well as for his team. He pushed everyone on the team to be their best. He prepared himself in a special way that made him a successful player.

He had multiple tour wins during his four year professional career. He was a much better player than me. He could hit every shot and make it look easy. He had the mental discipline that I lacked. I'm not sure how he did it, but he could let go of a bad hole and follow it up with a birdie. I, on the other hand, would always get upset if I bogeyed a hole.

James pushed me to be a better player. I was two years behind him in school. I would not have attempted college golf but I wanted to play with James on his team. I played my best golf during those two years and it was awesome. By the time he left school I was getting control of my emotions. I felt that he took it upon himself to prepare me to play my best.

He had a way of thinking his way around the course that came naturally. He shared with me how he thought and what he looked for when he was around the greens. This helped me understand my game much better, and as a result, I was able to average close to par during my college years. James' averages were the lowest in school history, and if he did not shoot below par, it was rare. I knew he was going to be a great professional. What I did not know was how short his career would be.

It was a tragedy that haunted me for years. James was in the prime of his career, married to his college sweetheart, and had a son who was only five years old, when his life was taken by cancer. During his fourth year on tour, James was diagnosed with stage two testicular cancer. How does this happen? I know testicular cancer is not rare for a male in his twenties, but how can a person, in the health that James was in, be so unfortunate to not beat this disease?

If there was any light in this, it was that Kevin was too young to understand what was going on. His mother felt that James would want to have Kevin play golf and asked me if I would take him under my wing. At the time, I felt like it was my duty to help in any way possible. I was more than happy to teach Kevin the game of golf. Over the years we developed a close relationship.

By the time Kevin was fifteen, he was playing as well as I ever did. I saw a lot of James in him. Just like his father, he could hit almost every shot, and, though he was at such a young age, it made me think he might have the future his dad did not get to have. But there was one thing that was different with Kevin; he did not have the mental toughness that James possessed. Kevin was more like me in that way.

I remember him playing in his first big junior tournament. He started out strong and in command. He was two under after the front nine, and it looked like he was going to run away from everyone. That all changed on the tenth green. He three putted for bogey and turned into Mr. Sourpuss. He talked to himself all the way to the eleventh tee, complaining about his missed putts. I could not believe it. How can he be so upset over one hole? But he was.

Soon, Kevin was on the bogey train, and he could not get off. It was not until the fifteenth hole that he finally made par. I could not believe it. I wondered if I was that bad when I was a junior player. He looked completely different on the front nine than he did on the back nine. Afterwards, I asked him how it went, and all he could talk about was that first bogey.

Kevin was able to calm down over the years. By the time he was coming out of college, his game was really coming into its own. He no longer had stretches of bad holes. He was not afraid to go for shots, and he played the risk/reward type of game. He thrived on shooting that low round. But now he finds himself in a difficult position. He cannot seem to win at the top level like he did in high school and college. He played his first two years on mini tours and made the pro tour on his third try. The problem he has had over the past four years has been getting that first big win.

After he returned home, we met for lunch and reviewed his career. "I'm not sure what to do anymore. I can't seem to play at the level I'm used to playing at, and it's taking a toll on me," said Kevin.

He was confused about his situation, and I did not have the answer for him. He has a week off before his next tournament. I just wish James was here. He would know what to say. We left that lunch without any answers. On the way home I could only think about how bad I felt for Kevin. It has been a long time since he has wanted to talk to me about his play. I have not really worked with him since his high school years. He has a good team around him, and my role now is to be his biggest fan. How am I going to help him?

FORE THE MIND - The Mental Program for Golf

Chapter 2

The Book

When I returned home, I started going through the box of things James had left for me. It had been a long time since I looked through this box. Most of the things were souvenirs and clippings from our junior and collegiate years of golf. I went through several scrapbooks and odds and ends of different things. James loved to keep ball markers and pencils from all the golf courses he played. I counted 103 pencils and 86 ball markers. What looked like a mess became the realization that these were memories of James' golf career.

I kept looking through the box, one thing after another. I was not sure what I was looking for. I guess I was hoping to find anything that would give me an answer to help Kevin, maybe a lucky charm or something. At the bottom of the box, I found it. I did not remember seeing this before. How could I overlook something like this? It was an old brown leather journal with curved edges, a dark stain on the back, and a leather strap around it.

As I opened the book up to the first page, a note fell out and landed on the floor. I reached down and picked up the note. It was a note to me that read the following:

FORE THE MIND - The Mental Program for Golf

Dear Bro,

It's been a long battle and my time has come. I am leaving you this journal that contains my secrets of the game of golf. These secrets aren't about the swing of golf, but rather my ability to have a mental advantage in competition. These are secrets I have come to discover throughout my career. I feel that this may inspire you to help others. In particular, Kevin.

If you find yourself reading this, then you know my career was cut short. I want Kevin to have an advantage over his competitors if he wishes to compete in golf. I never felt as though this was something I was going to share in a book or teach, but now I know these are things that players either don't know or take for granted.

The pages in the book are lessons of how I thought. I took a systematic approach to the game. Just as the golf swing requires specific guidelines to enhance a good swing, there are specific guidelines to the mental game as well. This is a system that helped give me mental consistency in competition and allowed me to take the emotion out of the game.

Please provide these secrets to Kevin when he is ready. Use any tactic you need to get this information across to him. I leave it up to you to decide when he is ready to learn these skills. These skills are the difference between winning and just competing.

Love you Bro, James

The beginning of the book was an introduction to James' approach on golf. I read the following pages with great interest and discovered that his approach to the game was quite different than mine. To me, golf is about competing and beating your opponent by the most strokes possible. Nothing feels better than shooting a low round and beating your competition by five or more strokes. If I birdie a hole, I'm on top of my game and feeling great. If I bogey a hole, I get frustrated and upset. This type of thinking was different for James. He explained his thoughts as follows.

Journal Entry

To understand the lessons I have written, you must first understand my approach to the game. Golf is an emotional sport with many variables. Everything in the game is designed to challenge you and disrupt your focus. Every hole is different. Some have room for a miss, while others place a premium on precision and accuracy. Every green is complex and unique with different contours and elevations, different looks from the fairways and bunker depth with different types of sand. You might play one championship course at 6900 yards, par 70 and another at 7500 yards at par 72.

This game makes you think all the time about something, and this is where the danger lies among players. Not only are the courses and holes different, but you have many different types of shots to master. You have a draw, fade, punch shot, putt, chip, and a slew of other shots that you need to pull off in order to have a good result. As you improve and get better, you may start to take some things for granted, and these things will come back and bite you in the butt.

To be able to play at your best is not easy. You must go against human nature. You must find out what everyone else is doing and go the other way, and once you discover that direction you must move fast. This type of thinking is something that is learned. It is not like the average person to control his or her thoughts on the golf course. In fact they do the opposite. They let the environment control their thoughts.

I first learned this approach to thinking in college. I noticed that every time a player didn't get the result they wanted, they got upset. In some cases the player would get really ticked off. This, for some reason, has become socially acceptable in the game. Why? What in the world can complaining about a bad shot do to help you in getting better results? It is not like you can go back and change the result. But this type of thinking and reaction is contagious.

I noticed I was starting to fall into this negative trap of thinking about what the environment was giving me. I was starting to complain about a poor round, then it resulted in a bad hole and then into a bad shot. I caught myself complaining about these bad shots and didn't realize that this thinking was affecting my score.

It was the second semester of my sophomore year that I noticed my scores going the wrong direction. My scoring average was getting worse, and I caught myself focusing on what was going wrong instead of thinking about what was going well. This had to change. I started to pay attention to my thought process and studied what my mindset was before and during every round. I found that when I focused on what I could control, my scores were almost always better than when I focused on the results. I decided at that moment I would control my thoughts and not let anyone or anything control my way of thinking.

The following pages are my approach to my thought processes and keys to my success as a player. This mental system is a process I developed over the years and I honestly feel this is what gave me an advantage over my competition. Too many players take the mental game for granted. They would play more consistently, and at their true potential, if they were better at controlling their thoughts. Think about it, can you control the weather? Can you control what other players do? Can you control the conditions of the course? No! But this is what players focus on; things they can't control. I went the other way.

I started to pay attention to the things I could control and what followed was a better performance, and lower scores. These techniques are not hard to understand, but implementing them is another story. It takes mental discipline to stay focused at critical moments in golf. The pre-shot routine is a good example.

All players go through a pre-shot routine. For most players, it's a rehearsed process they try to repeat on every shot. I look at the pre-shot routine as what a player is physically doing, and the Preload and Mental Program is what the player is mentally doing. I believe it's important to have a specific thought process that is defined and goes along with the pre-shot routine.

The strategy and the commitment phase of the shot are the two areas that describe the Preload. By having a specific and defined order of how a shot is broken down, it allows the player to make the correct decision and be able to commit to the shot with one hundred percent decisiveness. But this is just the beginning. A player needs to have a program that allows them to go from thinking to doing. The best shots you can make, as a player, are when you don't have to think about it. There must be a way in which a player can go from a conscious thought process to the subconscious action of hitting the shot. This journal is an explanation of the mental system that I used.

I wish had found this journal sooner. The things that James points out are spot on. I never thought of the pre-shot routine as being something more specific than a routine. James is stating that it is more than a routine, it's a mental process as much as a physical process.

What interested me most about this introduction was how much I did not know about James' golf game. I noticed James' consistent pre-shot routine in practice and in competition, but the discipline of the mental checklist was a revelation to me. I could not wait to read what James had left me.

Chapter 3

The Mental Checklist

After reading the journal, I felt like I was given the answer to helping Kevin with his game. I could not believe how James broke down the mental game. It was like a surgeon breaking down how he was going to execute a procedure on his patient. I read the pages with great interest and wished I had this insight during my career.

I wanted to share this with Kevin, but how? If he knew it was from me, he may not listen. Kevin would think, "After all, what does my uncle know?" How was I going to get this information to him in a way that he would take seriously? I wanted him to make a true effort in applying these techniques to his game? I thought about breaking down these lessons one at a time and presenting them to Kevin without him knowing it was me giving these lessons to him. I came up with the idea of putting lessons in a letter format and leaving them in his golf bag. Each week I planned to put a new lesson in his bag and watch his progress from a distance.

I watched Kevin from a distance with great anticipation, to see how he would respond to the first letter. While waiting for his caddie Alan, Kevin took his four and five irons out of his bag and began to swing and stretch to warm up before his training session. He would always swing two long irons to loosen up, similar to a baseball player swinging two bats to warm up. Once he finished his warm-up, he reached in the side pocket of his golf bag to get his glove. What he found was the first lesson in an envelope. He opened the envelope and read the following.

To Kevin,

I hope you find this letter to be of great interest. You have all the physical ability to play great golf, but you are missing one critical piece to breaking through and reaching your true potential. Golf is as much a mental game as it is a physical game. In fact, it is more mental the better you get.

In order for you to play at your best, you must pay close attention to where your mind is pointing. I have watched you play from a distance, and I can tell you that you must change the way you think on the course. You get sensitive over a poor shot. You also let the environment dictate how you think before every shot. Players set themselves up for success or failure by their thoughts before the action takes place. You must realize that the more you think about, talk about, and write about something happening, you improve the probability of that thing happening. This is a key principle to mental consistency, and mental consistency leads to technical consistency.

If you look at your game you will see a pattern. Every time you have a bad hole and you get upset, you follow it up with another bad hole. This doesn't have to be the case. You can change that by altering your thought pro-

cess. Over the next several weeks I will put a new lesson in your bag that will help you build a mental system to your golf game which will provide you an advantage in competition.

Your first lesson is a simple one and one that many players overlook. You must have a mental checklist before every shot. You must use this checklist every time you come up with your strategy of the shot. This checklist is very important because it greatly reduces error in your decision making.

You must organize your shots in the same order. Every shot has three things to consider: lie, conditions and yardage. You must have a specific order of these things, and you must process these things in that order every time. This greatly improves the probability of making a sound and confident decision of what type of club and shot to use. Without a specific order, you risk overlooking one of these areas and increase the probability of making a mistake. This mistake will cost you unnecessary shots.

The order of these things is not important. Some players will get the yardage first, while others will look at the lie first. The key is to find what order you think is most important. An example of this is lie, conditions, and yardage. Why the lie first? Because the lie will give you the options that are available to you. If the lie is bad, you are forced to consider a less desirable shot. This, in turn, will require you to use a different club.

The lie helps you decide your true target. If the ball is above your feet, it will go left of target. The opposite is true if the ball is below your feet. You must take this into account every time. This may sound elementary, but I am amazed at how many good players overlook this and miss shots because they align to the wrong target.

Secondly, you must look at the conditions. Conditions are everything. Such as wind, weather, elevation, and what's in front of you. These conditions are important because you have to take all of these things into consideration in order for you to make the correct choice of shot and club selection, along with your target.

Carefully determine how the wind will affect your ball, as well as how it will impact distance. Make a mental note and then calculate your yardage. This helps reduce the mistake of choosing the wrong club.

Three, calculate your yardage and make your adjustments from your lie and conditions. By getting the yardage last, it will help you calculate the correct yardage to your target. This improves the quality of the shot because you can now go into the shot with greater confidence. Practice this checklist and your decisions will become more effective.

Your Mentor

When Kevin finished the note, he folded it up and placed it in the same side pocket where he found it. When Alan met Kevin on the driving range, Kevin handed him the letter and said, "What's up with this?"

Alan replied, "I didn't write this! Why would I write you a letter when I could tell you in person. Who wrote it?"

"I thought it was you, man. Should we work on this or is this mumbo-jumbo stuff?"

Alan read the letter and paused before saying, "I think it makes sense. I can't say I've ever given much thought to having a specific order."

"That was my thought as well. I just didn't want to take advice from a phantom."

The Mental Checklist

"Phantom or not, good advice should be taken. Let's roll with it."

"What do you think is the first thing we should consider in a checklist? I'm thinking we should look at the lie first."

Alan thought about it for awhile and replied, "I calculate the yardage first. I have always been of the opinion that you take the lie into consideration, and my job is to calculate the yardage to the flag, front of the green and back of the green."

"OK, I will look at the lie while you get the yardage, and then we will talk about the conditions. This should keep us from making those dumb errors like mis-clubbing or hitting the wrong shot," replied Kevin.

For a solid week Kevin worked with Alan on his checklist. There was a tournament coming up that was perfect to see how this checklist would help Kevin. I cleared my calendar and went to watch him play.

On the first day, it was impressive to see how Kevin and Alan were on the same page. I walked alongside the ropes to try and hear every conversation throughout the round. During one shot, it was interesting to see how this checklist worked. It was a tough condition to read; the wind was blowing from right to left and into the players. Kevin drove the ball near the cart path. This made it easy to hear what Alan was telling him.

"We need to hit a fade at the flag." Alan said.

"What?! Are you serious? The wind is going right to left, and you want me to hit it at the flag?"

"Yes!" Replied Alan. "The wind is blowing right to left here, but take a close look at the flag. It's not moving. The tree tops behind the green are still. The wind condition down there is more important than what we feel and see here."

"OK, but if this doesn't work, I'm blaming you."

Kevin took his six iron and went into the shot aligning just left of the flag. He hit a beautiful fade that went right at the flag. The ball looked like it was going to land in the cup. It landed two feet in front of the hole and bounced two feet past the hole for an easy birdie putt.

On the way up to the green Alan explained to Kevin why he recommended that shot. Alan said, "So many players fail to really think about how the wind will affect the ball. I always look at the best wind indicators first. The flag, water, and trees are the best indicators of what the wind is doing, and just because it's blowing left to right at the ball doesn't mean the wind is blowing left to right at the target. This wind condition was coming more toward you and moving the ball right of the target. That's why a fade with the six iron was the perfect play. A seven iron would have come up short."

Alan made a great point. If it had not been for that checklist, he would not have had that opportunity to explain how he looks at the wind conditions. A player and caddie need to be on the same page. By having a consistent mental checklist of the things you are having to look at, you reduce mental error. You never want to be overlooking something that could be valuable in choosing the right decision.

Throughout the tournament Kevin made good decisions. He was not hitting the ball as well as he had in the past, but he managed to score well enough to have a top twenty finish. His inconsistency in his ball striking would have made it impossible for him to have a good finish with poor decision making. Good course management kept him from having those stray shots that cost players strokes. I was excited to see the change in Kevin's game, and I could not wait to get back to work on his next lesson.

On the way back home, I thought a lot about how James broke things down. He firmly believed that you could improve your score by reducing mental error. The checklist is the first part to this. I imagined how Kevin would have finished had he hit the ball well. He could have easily finished in the top ten, if not the top five. I thought about how many times I missed a shot because I didn't have a consistent way to break the shot down. If this allowed Kevin the ability to stay competitive, how much better will he play with the other lessons that will follow?

Chapter 4

Commitment

As soon as I got home, I worked on putting together the next lesson. I had a good feeling of how things were looking and could not wait to get the next lesson together. James had explained in his journal that you must commit to the decision. I thought this was obvious. Who does not commit to their decision? After going back and reading his notes, I realized that making a decision and truly committing to that decision are two different things.

We all make decisions and go with them. Many times we make choices and do not think twice about what the results will be. Will I like the outcome? Is this the best decision to make? Are there better alternatives? We do not really think about how our decision will impact us. James' view was we must consider how the decision could impact us.

Journal Entry

You must carefully choose your shot, and then, and only then, can you commit to the shot 100 percent. So many times a player will choose the shot and take the club out of the bag and go through the motions of the swing. This is a terrible mental mistake. The player must mentally rehearse while physically conducting the practice swing. Look at the shots players mess up. Is it the hard shots? No, it is the easy ones. Why? Because the player takes the easy shot for granted and doesn't commit to the shot with the same level of effort as the hard shots.

In order to have technical consistency, you must first have mental consistency. This is especially true in golf. How can players expect to have a consistent physical game when their mind is inconsistent? They can't, but that is exactly what players do. They make a decision and go through the motions, never committing to the shot. The players are hoping they are making the right decisions, but hope is not were you want to be. In order for players to execute good shots, on a consistent basis, they need to commit to their decisions.

The idea is to have a mental system that allows you to trust your game. Doubt is your enemy on the course. Trust is your friend. You can't trust your decisions if you don't commit to the shot. This means that you must be 100% decisive about the choice you made. It doesn't matter if the decision you make is the correct one. What matters most is that you commit to that decision. By having a 100% "I'm sold attitude", it allows you to go into the shot with more confidence. This attitude is what makes the commitment phase easier to trust.

My advice is to consciously program what you want the Subconscious Mind to do. This is accomplished when players take their practice swing. You must mentally and physically feel and execute the shot you want to have. This provides a vivid imprint into the Self-Image and improves the probability of executing the shot you want, therefore getting the result you desired. This can't be achieved with a half-hearted approach. Every shot requires and deserves the same amount of attention and effort.

Notice that I am not using the term effort to mean giving it all you have or giving it 110%. I am stating that the level of effort you give each shot must have the same amount of effort during the commitment phase. This allows the practice swings to be performed consistently instead of falling into the trap of going through the motions. Committing to the shot is a key ingredient to playing consistent golf.

I started to realize that Kevin was not committing to the shots the way James described in the journal. James took an approach that I never noticed in him. He was really committed to making the mental game a priority in golf. I needed to get the point across to Kevin. I took this information and wrote down the second lesson for Kevin.

To Kevin,

You've made the first lesson look easy. The discipline you displayed in getting the checklist down and staying with it shows how serious you are with making the mental game a priority. The last lesson was the first part of the Preload. The Preload is the mental part of the pre-

shot routine. It is the part of the preparation of the shot that is done consciously. Golf requires you to think. If you don't have a mental system to control your thoughts, you will ultimately make mental mistakes.

Last time I broke down the strategy of the shot. This time I'll break down the second part of the Preload, commitment. After you have made your decision, you must commit to the shot you choose. At times you get lazy and make half hearted practice swings. In order to play at your best, you must give the same amount of effort on every shot.

Ask yourself, "What is the most important shot in golf?" I'm sure you are thinking "the next one." The reality is that all shots are important. They are all equally important. You can't afford to take any shot for granted, nor can you afford to give any shot too much thought. Your job is to make the best decision you can and commit to it. Every shot requires you to have the same effort level.

Taking shots for granted leads to carelessness. Carelessness leads to mistakes. Giving too much thought about the shot leads to over-thinking. Over-thinking leads a player to over-trying. Over-trying is the number one reason good players don't play well in competition. They let the environment pull their focus. Placing too much importance on the shot causes you to try instead of trust. You don't want to make things happen, you want to let things happen.

Letting things happen means you trust the decision you have chosen, and you commit to that shot 100%. This is what the Preload is all about. The best way to do this is to break down your practice swings into two parts.

First, focus on your practice swing, or swings, on the

technical aspects of executing the shot you have chosen. Your focus is on how to execute the shot you want. Take a slow swing and harness the move you need to make to hit the shot well. Sometimes you will need to take an extra practice swing to imprint the correct move.

Second, feel the shot you want to make. Focus on tempo and rhythm of the shot. You want to have the feeling of confidence with the shot and trust that this is the best shot for you. This technique works because you are going from trying to trusting. You are trying to feel the execution of the shot, and following that up with the feeling of rhythm and tempo.

By taking time to mentally and physically rehearse the shot you want before you address the ball, you provide a mental imprint to increase the probability of hitting the shot you've chosen. Committing to the shot is vital to having mental consistency. This will help you build confidence in the decision you made and put you in a better position to getting the result you desire.

Use this technique to master committing to the shot. Once you have mastered this commitment phase of the Preload, you will be able to go into every shot with the same amount of confidence.

Your Mentor

It was a Tuesday afternoon when Kevin reached in the side pocket and retrieved the second lesson. After reading the lesson, he took out his little notepad and wrote a note to himself. The note read, "Divide your practice swings into two parts. On your first swing, execute the technique of that swing. On the second swing, feel the tempo and rhythm of the swing."

That afternoon Kevin spent two hours on the driving

range, practicing his commitment phase of the shot. He spent that time alternating targets and going through his Preload. He started with strategy and decision making. He followed that up with his practice swings and then hit the shot. He would pick a target and choose the shot he wanted to make, then go through his system. He did this for a draw, then a fade, then a punch shot, etc. He mixed his shots up and committed to every shot. He made the exact move in his practice swing he needed to make in the real shot.

What followed was Kevin's ability to dial in on the targets on the driving range. Selecting the driver, he would take two practice swings and rip a perfect shot at his target. He changed to a nine iron and made two slow technical swings, followed by one feel swing and hit a little fade to a tree. He alternated shots and kept hitting great shot after great shot. He started to make the game look easy.

Later in the week, Kevin asked me to play a round of golf with him. He sounded excited and wanted to share with me his new techniques that he was working on. When I met him at the course, he was all smiles. While we were waiting on the first tee box, he shared with me the letters he had received in his bag.

"I received a letter in my bag a couple of weeks ago, and it was a lesson on the mental game of golf. Actually, it was a breakdown of something I had taken for granted, and I applied it to my game last week during the tournament. I was surprised at how many shots I might have been losing just because I wasn't paying close attention to the process of decision making. On Tuesday, the second letter was a lesson on commitment. I always thought I was committing to my shots, but after practicing this over the last few days, I have realized how much I wasn't doing."

Kevin went on and on about how simple and powerful the

lessons were to his game. On the fourth hole he turned to me and asked the following question: "I wonder who could be leaving these lessons for me?"

My reply was quick and simple, "Who knows?"

Chapter 5

Preload for Putting

As I sat down to think about the next lesson I wanted to share with Kevin, I realized I had given him only part of the answer. James described that the Preload was different for putting vs. ball striking. In his view, they were two separate parts of the game. Putting is completely separate from ball striking. They are two different types of shots and both deserve a different thought process in Preloading the shot.

In putting your lie is consistent. You can clean the ball and place it back to its spot; therefore, you don't have the same lie, conditions and yardage as in ball striking. You must look at putting differently. You must change the mental checklist in putting so that you focus on the read and speed of the putt.

Putting should be the best part of every golfer's game, according to James. James put it this way: "You will have a putt on every hole, except on those occasions when you have a hole in one or you chip one in. Other than that, the shots are always changing from tee to green, but once you are on the green, consistency on how to view the shot becomes an advantage."

According to the journal, a player must define when he is

in the preloading phase. This starts when the player begins to gather information about the putt. The player is making decisions about what he has to do to make the putt. Speed and read become the primary focus. You cannot just read a putt and expect to make it; you must take into account how much speed you want to give it. Once you start gathering information about the shot, you do not want to have any distractions.

If you want to increase the chances of scoring, you must make putts. Putting has the advantage of allowing you to line up the ball in a desired manner. Putting also has a disadvantage; the closer you are to the hole, the more you are tempted to think about score. When looking at a five foot putt for par, it becomes difficult not to think about this shot being for par. If you make it you have par; if you do not, you have bogey.

When score is staring you in the face, you must have a mental system to keep the score out of your mind and keep process the main focus. This is done by organizing how you read the putt. Almost everyone reads the putt from behind the ball, and in some cases that is correct. But you also need to get a second look at the read you are trying to define. Always get a minimum of two looks from two separate angles. James always read the putt from behind the ball, and the second look from the low side of the break.

When reading the putt from behind the ball, you get a good idea of what you think the line should be. This is not a true indicator of what will happen, it is only one indicator. In order to make the best educated guess, a player must look at the putt from other angles. The best angle is from the low side of the break. This angle is a better indicator because from the low side of the line you see everything. The slope is more obvious and you can make the adjustment to your line from your initial indicator, behind the ball.

If players can confirm the read, they can now go into the

commitment phase with confidence. If they are still in doubt, they need to get a third angle of the read. The best option for the third angle of reading the putt is from behind the hole. This will give you the best information on which line looks best: the one behind the ball, or the one from the low side. Once you have this information, you must be one hundred percent sold on your decision about what you think the read looks like.

Making a good read is important, but committing to your read is more important. It does not matter if you are right or not on your read. There are many times a putt will fool you, but if you do not commit to your read, you will not be able to commit to your putt. By not committing to the putt, you will put yourself into a second-guessing mentality. This mentality will always fail you. It does not matter if you are right or not, it only matters that you commit to the putt.

What I learned from James is that committing to the putt starts with your first look at the putt. Once you get all your information, you can now commit to that decision and focus on the putting stroke and the speed of the putt. I took this information and wrote out the next lesson for Kevin.

To Kevin,

The first two lessons were about how to prepare for the shot. Now it's time to break down the putt. Putting also has a Preload phase, like ball striking, but there are some differences you need to consider.

When walking up to the putt, you must establish when and where you start to gather information about the putt. This starting point is important because it draws your focus to the task at hand. Once you start to gather information about the putt, you are in the Preloading phase of the putt. Your focus must be on that putt and nothing else. There should be no more thinking about the previous shot, the other players, spectators, etc. Just like an approach shot you must have a specific order to strategize the putt.

By having a specific order, it will ensure that you will not take the initial read for granted. This type of thinking is often overlooked by better players. When players can score and have experience, they can get caught on relying on experience too much. This often leads to misreading the putt. This type of mistake would not have happened earlier in their career.

Think about the order. Where do you start to get your information? The following is an example of what the order could be for putting. First, take a look at the read from behind the ball. This is typically a good start for most players, but it should not be the only look you take. Once you have the initial information about the read, you need to get a confirmation look.

Second, go to the low side of the line. If you are putting and you see the break going left to right, you want to look at the severity of the break. The best angle to see this break is from the low side. By looking at the line from below the break, you can see the slope of the green and get a better idea of how much the putt will move. This second look will improve the probability of making a good read and getting the correct line.

Third, if you can't confirm the read from the low side, you must get a third look. This is when you go behind the hole and read the putt from there. You will see that one of the other two looks is a better read and be able to confirm the line you want to take. This order allows you to make the best read possible and provides confidence in

Preload for Putting

the decision that is being made. Now it's easier to commit to the shot.

When watching you play, you rarely take a third look. On easier putts, this is acceptable, but there are times that you should take more time to really study the line and make sure it's the correct read. A good indicator that you have the read and speed down is that you will rarely miss the putt on the low side of the hole. You must give yourself every possible chance to make the putt.

Once you have made the decision, you must turn your focus on the speed of the green and the putting stroke you want to make during your practice strokes. This will allow you to go into the putt with confidence. If you look at the top putters in the game, you will see that most of them take their practice strokes next to the ball. This allows them to keep this feeling throughout the putt.

It's not important how many practice strokes you take. It doesn't have to be consistent from one putt to the next. What's important is you mentally and physically rehearse the putt you want to make and trust this is the correct shot to execute. Never go into a putt with doubt. Always stay confident in your decision. This can only be accomplished by committing to the putt and doing all the work in the Preload.

When taking your practice strokes, have your mind on the specific task you want to accomplish. First, focus on getting the correct stroke. Second, focus on the speed of the putt. Third, focus on feeling confident. Mentally rehearse that you execute the putt well and see it go on line. If you are able to execute that putt and you made the correct read, there is only one possible outcome: the ball will go in the hole.

The main point to this lesson is to avoid getting caught

up in making or not making the putt. Outcome thoughts will not help you in this situation. You must focus on executing the shot you want and be totally committed to your decision about that shot. Trust is what allows you to score. Trusting your decision and committing to the shot will allow you to let the shot happen. You never want to make the shot happen, you only want to let it happen. This starts with having a clear and defined order of how you will commit to your decision on the greens.*

Your Mentor

I was not sure how this lesson would go over with Kevin. A player at his level should know the things I am suggesting, but if I learned anything from James' writings it was even the best can get off track and cost themselves unnecessary strokes. I truly believed this was what was happening with Kevin.

Over the last few weeks Kevin had made some strides in his approach to his game, and I felt confident he would continue to make progress. I was worried he might take my comments about his game the wrong way. He gets ahead of himself at times and this is a mental mistake that costs him strokes in every tournament.

Later that week, I took my wife out for dinner. We just wanted to get out and have a nice time. It was a Thursday evening and neither of us wanted to stay home and cook, so off to the steakhouse we went. This little steakhouse had become a favorite place for us, it was the kind of place you could sit back and kick up your feet. As you walk throughout the restaurant you hear cracking noises from all the peanut shells on the floor.

There was a corner booth we liked to sit at and as luck

Preload for Putting

would have it, it was available. As we followed the host to the corner booth, I saw Alan sitting at a table by himself. I wondered if he had seen Kevin this week. When we sat down I pointed over to Alan and said to my wife, "Look, Alan's here!"

She replied, "Is he by himself? We should see if he wants to join us."

Neither my wife, nor I, like to eat alone. So I got up and went over to invite Alan to join us. "What are you doing here, stranger?"

Alan looked up with a surprised look on his face. "Well what are you doing here? Where's Kim?" Alan replied.

"She's over there, and we wanted to know if you would join us," I said.

"Absolutely, that would be great. I haven't seen you guys in a while."

As we sat down to order, I asked Alan how things were going. He was all smiles. I had not seen him this happy in years. He told us about how his brother was doing and how he was, but what really got my attention is when he talked about Kevin. He told us he had been working with Kevin this week and shared the following with us: "I've known Kevin for eight years, and this is my third year to caddie for him. I see a spark in him I haven't seen before. He started to get these letters in his bag. They're like mini lessons on golf and how you should think. At first I thought it was bogus, but it has really helped us increase our communication with each other. You know how the last tournament went? It was the first time he really took my advice to heart, and it was because of that letter. It forced him to break down a strategy for each shot. It was great."

I jumped in and asked, "How is he doing this week?"

"Oh, this week has been all about the greens. He has really

focused on breaking down the putt in a specific order. He used to walk around the green and look at the putt and go with it. This week he has taken a different approach to reading putts. He wants me to read the putt but only give him advice when he asks for it. I tend to look at my yardage book, see what notes I have made about the green, and then read the putt with that information in mind, telling him my thoughts. I think I assumed he always wanted my input.

Kevin is approaching the putt with a specific order. He first marks his ball and steps back to get his initial read. He then goes to the low side of the break to see the slope of the green. Sometimes he will go behind the hole, but not always. It's been interesting to see a consistent pattern to how he reads the green.

For me, this is great. I don't have to remind him about things. I know he's taking each putt with the same importance. It has taken pressure off me. I can focus on what I see and only give him advice when he asks for it. I think I have been guilty in the past of giving him too much to think about. Sometimes it's better to just let the player play. I can't wait to see how this new strategy works in a tournament, but that won't be until the end of the month."

I smiled and said, "Is he feeling more confident in his game?"

"Absolutely!" Said Alan. "You can see the confidence in his face. I really think he will have a better year. He might even win! I think he just needs to trust himself."

I couldn't agree more with what Alan said. Kevin had the ability to compete against anyone. If he could just get some consistency with his game and trust himself, he could shoot low scores. I couldn't wait to see him break through.

Chapter 6

The Mental Program

The next morning I opened James' journal and started reading where I had left off. I was curious to see how James continued his thought process throughout the shot. So far things seemed to be in a logical, specific order. This type of mental system seemed to be so easily organized and simple. It just amazed me how I overlooked some of these things when I was competing.

I do not remember James using these techniques when he played. How could I have missed these steps in his game? I was curious to find out how James narrowed his thought process before hitting the shot. I have always had an active mind throughout my golf career. Even today I struggle with controlling my thoughts. I just don't see how a player can go from thinking about the shot to just doing it without thinking about what the result might be before hitting the shot.

The Preload is all about thinking about the shot and trying to come up with the best strategy to get the best desired outcome. Even the commitment phase is results based. I'm trying to commit to the shot I have chosen so I can perform that in the action phase of hitting the shot. What I was about to discover is how James went from having an active mind in the Preload to having a singular focus just before the action of hitting the shot.

As I continued to read and study James' writings, I realized things started to take a turn in his thought process. According to James, a player must control his thoughts all the way up to the time he hits the shot. He stated that you do not want to think during the shot. All the thinking is done beforehand, and the thought process needs to be consistent on every shot. The following is how he broke it down.

Journal Entry

I have spent hours trying to figure out a systematic way to transfer my mind from a conscious thought to a subconscious action. I have created a program that has given me a huge advantage over my competition. I call this thought process the "Mental Program." While my competition is over the ball trying to think about the shot they are going to hit, I run a specific set of thoughts that make the transfer from conscious to subconscious possible.

Think about the times you play. How many times do you have thoughts that creep into your head while you're over the ball? How many times does that thought change? On one three foot putt you might think, "I got this." On another three foot putt you might think, "Don't miss this." In both examples you are faced with a three foot putt, but the thoughts are different while you're over the ball. Your thoughts should be consistent. You must have a consistent thought process in order to get consistent results.

How can players expect to have technical consistency if they don't have mental consistency? If a player doesn't have a consistent thought process to occupy the Conscious Mind on each and every shot, he will not be able to duplicate the necessary Subconscious skill. When I realized I can control my thoughts, I realized I can improve my technical consistency by running a consistent Mental Program. The Mental Program is a series of thoughts that, when pictured, will trigger the Subconscious to perform the appropriate action. This action is the shot I programmed in the commitment phase of the Preload.

This allowed me the ability to trust what I Preloaded and accept the shot. The difference between the Preload and the Mental Program is the Mental Program is always the same. It requires great discipline to perform this technique on a consistent basis. The Mental Program is broken down into three parts: Point of Initiation, Point of Alignment, and Point of Focus.

The starting point of the Mental Program is referred to as the Point of Initiation. This is a physical trigger that starts the Mental Program. I always tapped the club on the ground before going into the shot. This is extremely important because it not only identifies the starting point, but also keeps the player from rushing into the shot. This step encourages a consistent tempo and rhythm.

This physical trigger can be anything from twirling the club, to tugging your shirt, to taking a deep breath, to tapping the club on your foot. It's not important what trigger you select, but it must be consistent. The Point of Initiation must be the same for every similar shot. If the Point of Initiation changes from the tee shot to the approach shot, how can a player expect to have a consistent program?

After the Point of Initiation, the player now goes to the second step of the Mental Program: the Point of Alignment. The Point of Alignment is the series of thoughts and actions of the player while aligning his shot. Many players are inconsistent in this area. Sometimes they take one look, other times two or three looks. That's not consistent. The player must define what each look is for and commit to the same process for every golf shot.

This part of the Mental Program should be easy, but for many players it's not. When you break down each step of the alignment, it allows for the Conscious Mind to be engaged in the same thought process every time. This is what consistency is all about. Without defining what you should think about, you allow the environment to influence your thoughts. The environment is always changing. Remember this, you can't master something if it's not defined, but once you define something, you can now master it. After you have mastered something you can then expect to duplicate that task. With duplication comes consistency and with consistency comes trust. That is what the Mental Program allows.

The final stage of the Mental Program is the Point of Focus. The Point of Focus is the most critical of the three steps in the Mental Program. The reason is that this is the last few seconds before the shot is executed. At this point, a player cannot afford to have passing thoughts that enter his mind. These passing thoughts often cause players to have a poor swing, and therefore get a poor result.

I remember having the thought, right before I took the club back: "You need this one, don't mess up." This thought never helped me hit a good shot. In fact, it did the opposite. It caused me to have bad shots. I was determined to create my own thought process that would keep these passing thoughts out of my head right before I hit the shot. By implementing the Mental Program, the passing thoughts went away. As a result, I became a more consistent player who shot lower scores on a regular basis.

To help with this final thought in the Point of Focus, use the following criteria. This criteria consists of five things. First, the thought must occupy your Conscious Mind. Second, the thought must transfer power to the subconscious. This means you should have the feeling of letting the shot happen and not making it happen. Third, keep the thought simple. Golf is already complicated, the last thing a player needs to do it to make the Mental Program complicated. Fourth, it must be duplicable. Finally, it needs to be player specific.

You can't expect to have a consistent swing of the golf club if your thoughts are always changing. It is up to the player to define what he should think about. Once this is done the player needs to stick with that program. This provides mental consistency and therefore allows for technical consistency. Once I made this Mental Program a consistent part of my golf game, my whole game became more consistent.

What James had written really resonated with me. I never knew he had a specific thought process when he was over the ball. All this time I was worrying about how well I ran my routine, but I never considered my mind needed to be consistent like my routine. I had to make this simple and straightforward for Kevin to understand. I felt that this could be the difference in Kevin winning compared to just competing.

Chapter 7

The Point of Initiation

As I started to organize my lessons for Kevin, I wondered why I had not thought about this sooner. I remembered playing with James in college and watching him on the pro tour, but I never noticed this Mental Program he was describing in his journal. I tried to recall his Point of Initiation, but I could not remember him tapping the club before walking into the shot. Was it really necessary to have this Point of Initiation like James explained?

According to James, this is extremely important. I decided to test this Point of Initiation out before writing the next lesson for Kevin. I took my wife to the golf course and asked her to watch me run my routine. I instructed her to pay close attention to the physical trigger, which was twirling the club. I asked her to count how many times I stepped toward the ball after I finished the twirl. She kept stats on how many good shots I had compared to bad shots and made a note when I performed the physical trigger well. After practicing this on the driving range, I was ready to put this to the test.

I played the round, and as usual, I had some great holes and some bad ones. I play every week, but my game isn't as consistent as it once was. I was happy with my overall score, but more importantly, I wanted to see the notes my wife made during the round. Being a college player herself, she would have a unique perspective. As we sat in the clubhouse she began to explain what she saw.

"It was very interesting watching you play today. On the first three holes you did really well on the Point of Initiation, but after that you began to get inconsistent."

I replied, "I thought I did a good job on making sure I did the twirl after my practice swings. How could I be different after the first three holes?"

"You performed this task well on the tougher shots. It was the easy ones you were inconsistent on. For example, the fifth hole is the easiest par four on the course. You made the comment, "I got this", as you pulled out your driver. This shot was one of your worst shots of the day, and you twirled the club as you were taking your first step to address the ball. You are supposed to finish the twirl before you take that first step."

My wife showed me her notes which solidified the case for James' theory. On the majority of the shots I hit well, I performed the twirl perfectly. On the majority of the shots I hit poorly, I did not perform the Point of Initiation correctly. This was an eye opener for me. I did not think this really would make a difference. How could this be? How could something so simple be of such importance?

As my wife and I continued to discuss this, I realized one important thing. When I did not perform this starting point of the Mental Program, my routine was faster and my swing was quicker. It hit me! James was brilliant. The body follows the mind, and if you get quick in the thought process, you will improve the probability of being quick in the swing. By having a physical trigger to focus on, you eliminate the chance of approaching the ball prematurely.

The Point of Initiation

This starting point will improve the consistency of the Mental Program. If the start point is not performed consistently, why would the rest of the Mental Program be consistent? This made it easier for me to break down the next lessons for Kevin. I cannot wait for him to notice what I experienced.

To Kevin,

I am excited about the progress you are making. Now you are ready for the next step. I know you have a pre-shot routine you run on every shot, but this routine is not always consistent. Over the next three lessons, I will break down a process that will explain what you should focus on during your routine. This process is called a Mental Program. A player needs to have consistent thoughts during his routine. Without a defined thought process, you risk the probability of having passing thoughts. These passing thoughts are often negative and cause poor results.

The Mental Program consists of three parts: a start, a middle and an end. The first part is the lesson for today. Like anything in life, you must have a starting point, and the starting point for the Mental Program is called Point of Initiation. This is a physical trigger that is done after the commitment phase of the Preload. This starts the Mental Program.

The physical trigger is a subtle move that a player makes that says "I'm ready." It could be twirling the club, tapping the club on the ground, taking a deep breath, tugging your shirt, or pointing the club to the target and bringing it down to your side. It is important you decide on one thing and you do this for every shot. You must also perform this task before you approach the shot.

This will keep you from rushing into a shot and getting quick over the ball.

Think about the times you play your best. Everything is working together, and you are in a duplicable rhythm. The Mental Program promotes this rhythm and will allow you to have better consistency in your game. If the Point of Initiation is not consistent, how can you expect the rest of the routine to be consistent? You must have a starting point that defines when the Mental Program begins. This is your task for the week. Discover what physical trigger you want to use and duplicate that on every shot.

Your Mentor

Like clockwork, Kevin pulled out his small notepad and made a note. He wrote, "*Define the start point.*" He went on with his normal training session and did not work on the lesson that day. The next morning he showed up early. I was sitting outside the clubhouse drinking my morning coffee when I noticed Kevin walking by with one club in his hand.

I yelled, "What's that?"

His response was short and to the point: "Seven iron and a notepad, going to work."

He spent the next two hours on the driving range hitting that seven iron. From my view it looked like he was practicing his routine, but he was doing more than that. He was working on his Point of Initiation. He was trying out different things. He spent twenty minutes twirling the club, just like I did. He picked up his notepad and made some notes. He spent the next twenty minutes tapping the club on the ground as his Point of Initiation. I think he tried six or seven different things that morning, making notes after each one.

When Kevin finished, he left for the day. I would not see him for the next three days. My curiosity was getting to me. What did he settle on? What was he using for his Point of Initiation? I thought twirling the club would be perfect. I guess it is player specific. James was making the case that the physical trigger is the priority. What the player does for the physical trigger is his preference. If this is the case, it makes sense why Kevin spent so much time on this lesson. He was personalizing the physical trigger to suit him.

On Friday, Kevin was playing on the course with his usual playing group. During the weeks he was not competing, he would play with a couple of other tour players who were taking the week off. There were about five of them, and every Friday two or more would play the morning round together. It was an idea that Matt came up with. Matt is two years ahead of Kevin and is a good player. He is considered by many to be the best player on tour without a tour victory. He always thought you should play with the best players every week. So one day he pitched the idea to Kevin, Steve, Tommy, and Greg. They all thought is was a great way to stay in competition mode.

This week Kevin was playing with Matt and Steve. Matt had all the physical tools to play against anyone; there was not a shot he could not hit. Watching him play was similar to watching a roller coaster ride. He would go on these birdie stretches but then have a stretch of bad holes. He managed to finish near the top but never won a tournament. It's amazing how a player can perform in situations like he does while at the same time lacking the confidence that he can pull off the victory.

Unlike Matt, Steve had won on tour. He did not possess the same ability Matt did, but he never lacked confidence in his game. If there was a downfall in Steve's game it would be handling pressure. He had two victories on tour and both were without pressure ending putts that had to be made. He won his first tournament by shooting the low round on the final day and moving up eleven spots to win the tournament by two strokes. The second tournament he won was the best four day performance of his life. Steve's problem was he had not been able to win when he was in contention on the final day. He let the pressure get to him.

I decided to watch them play from a distance to see if I could determine Kevin's Point of Initiation. During the first three holes, I could not tell what he was using as a physical trigger. I had my binoculars focused on him, and I still had a hard time figuring out what he was doing to start the Mental Program.

On the fourth hole, during his approach shot, I figured it out. Kevin would keep the club in his left hand as he looked at his target then would move his right hand forward and back. It looked like a gunslinger move, only more subtle.

Throughout the rest of the day he stayed consistent with his Point of Initiation. How could he pick this up so fast? I was not that consistent. I knew he was a professional, but he was still my nephew. I was impressed and could not wait to put the next lesson together. How much better could he get once this Mental Program became a part of his game?

Chapter 8

The Point of Alignment

James made one thing clear in his writings, you must be consistent with your Mental Program. But what does it mean to be consistent? He wrote that being consistent is the number one priority in the game of golf. This is how he put it.

> *Journal Entry*
>
> Mental consistency is primary. It's the number one thing a player needs to have in order to play at his highest level. When players are playing well, they have mental consistency because their focus is all positive. But look what happens when a good player is not playing well. His body language changes, and thoughts are inconsistent. I made a conscious decision to control my thoughts and go the other way.
> When I developed my Mental Program, I made sure I defined my thought process. I defined what I focused on for every step, both physically and mentally. How can a player expect to be consistent

when their thoughts are inconsistent? Watch players and you will be amazed how many of them are different in his pre-shot routine. I believe the reason is because the pre-shot routine is not defined.

The pre-shot routine describes what the player is physically doing, but it doesn't describe, or define, what the player is thinking. This is why I break down the steps in the Preload and Mental Program. The Preload varies because each shot is unique. Therefore, the strategy of each shot changes. The Mental Program, however, is different because it needs to be consistent. These are the last thoughts before the action. You must define the thoughts in the Mental Program. If the thoughts are not defined you will not have mental consistency.

It's easy to define what the Point of Initiation is because it's always something physical and it takes only a second to do. The second part of the Mental Program is much more difficult to define. The Point of Alignment describes the steps and thoughts of the player while he is over the ball. When I observed players, I noticed that they didn't perform this part of their routine the same. Sometimes they take two looks at the target, sometimes three looks. Why? Why aren't the looks consistent? It's because their thought process isn't consistent.

In order to have consistency, you must define what you do and why you do it. For me, I had to get my club aligned to the target before I set my feet. I often see players do both at the same time. This is a critical mental error on their part. The Conscious Mind can only think about one thing at a time. How can the player focus on properly

The Point of Alignment

> aligning the club at the same time he is aligning his feet? He can't! His focus has to go to one or the other. This type of approach often causes the player to align off target. My approach changed once I realized that I couldn't focus on two things at once.
>
> In my approach, I walked into the shot looking at my target and then set my club head to that target. I took my first look and confirmed my line before I set my feet. My focus was organized in a step-by-step manner. First, align club head to the target. Second, focus on setting feet. Third, look at target to confirm alignment. This may sound simple, but it's not. It's hard to make yourself follow a specific program and trust that the shot will be good. When I mastered my Mental Program, I became more consistent in my play and my performance improved. When performance improves, so does the score.

Wow, James was right. This was interesting to me. I never focused on how many looks a player takes. I never paid attention to how many looks I took. I always focused on getting comfortable over the ball. What I did not realize was how much my routine differed from shot to shot. This was something I just took for granted.

The next day I was scheduled to play with a former college teammate, Andy, and two other players. Sam and Curt were mini tour players trying to make it on the pro tour. Andy and I enjoyed playing with younger players. They always pushed us to stay competitive. Nothing feels better than beating a good player who is almost half your age. It keeps my competitive juices flowing.

During the round I took notice of how many looks each

player took. I paid close attention to see if there was any consistency with these guys. As you might guess, Andy was not consistent in his routine. He had a routine, but it was not consistent. On some shots, he took more time compared to others. This did not surprise me, considering neither of us compete anymore. What surprised me was the inconsistency of Sam and Curt.

Sam had a routine similar to the one James described in the journal. He was fast. He walked up to the ball, took one look at the target, and set his feet, and took a second look before he hit the shot. What surprised me about Sam was as soon as he hit a bad shot, the next shot's routine changed. He took more looks than normal. I realized what James was talking about in the beginning of his writings. Players are more concerned with the result than the process. Sam's routine changed because of the results. As the round went on both his routine and his scoring became inconsistent.

Curt was different. He was all over the place. Sometimes he took practice swings and sometimes he did not. He took extra time on easy shots, and on some harder ones he looked hurried. I could not believe how well he played considering he did not have a consistent routine. He was hitting the ball well. On hole thirteen he made a comment that he felt like he could not miss. He was just on. This made me wonder, "How would he play if he was not hitting the ball so well?" Like many players, he feeds off his play. When he plays well, he is not afraid to go low, but on the days he is not playing well he cannot produce anything close to a good score.

It was a very different day for me. I had fun and played well, but the real pleasure of the day was seeing how the other players ran their routine. All of us can shoot par or better, but the young guys compete. I thought they would be better at running a pre-shot routine. They were not. It proves James'

The Point of Alignment

point, the mental game is the priority! Most players are focusing on the shot when they should be focusing on the process of the shot. That evening I wrote Kevin's next lesson.

To Kevin,

You created a unique and interesting Point of Initiation last week. This shows that you are taking these lessons seriously. Now comes the hard part. In this lesson you must define the second step to the Mental Program, the Point of Alignment. The Point of Alignment is a series of thoughts and steps to align the shot. You must make this consistent.

When you watch your competition, you will notice most of them are not consistent with their routine. The most inconsistent part occurs when the player is over the ball. Players vary in how many looks they take. Sometimes they will look at the target two times, while other times they will take three looks or more. How many looks are you taking? Do you know the purpose of each look? This must be answered in order for you to have a consistent thought process over the ball.

Most players do not define what they think about while over the ball. They focus on the shot. If you perform the Preload correctly, you don't need to focus on the shot while over the ball. You must focus on the process of letting the shot happen. This is done by minimizing the amount of thinking. The Point of Alignment is the answer.

This part of the Mental Program starts after the Point of Initiation. When you address the ball and start your alignment, make sure you have the steps defined. An example is to align the club head to the target, then focus on setting your feet, confirm the alignment with another look at the target and then hit the shot. The focus is on the steps.

If you can define these steps and focus only on them, you will have mental consistency. Mental consistency will help produce technical consistency, which will, in turn, provide you with more consistent scores. This process means your timing and rhythm will be the same. Take time to define the process that fits you best. Remember, you can only think about one thing at a time. If you are trying to focus on two things at once, you will be forced to choose between the two. Make sure the order is defined and follow it every time.

Your Mentor

On the following Tuesday, Kevin did not wait to read his lesson on the driving range. While in the locker room he retrieved the lesson from the bag and took it to the bar area to read it. As he sat at the corner table by himself, he pulled out his little notepad with a black pen and placed them on the table. After he finished reading his lesson, he wrote down the following notes: *Work with Alan on alignment. Ask him how consistent my alignment process is.* He then got up and went to practice.

The next two weeks were important for Kevin. It had been a while since his last tournament, but he was going on a three week tournament stretch in two weeks. To help him prepare, he scheduled time to work with Alan on Wednesday and Thursday.

On Wednesday morning Alan showed up at the course to work with Kevin. He was excited to get back into competition mode. Like most caddies on tour, you are not making money if you are sitting at home. He only gets paid when Kevin gets

The Point of Alignment

paid. Kevin's plan was to work with Alan on the course and go through some tournament rehearsal training.

When Alan met Kevin on the driving range, Kevin had a different attitude. He was serious and straightforward with his questions for Alan.

"How consistent is my pre-shot routine?" said Kevin.

"What? No 'Hello' or 'How's it going Alan?'" replied Alan.

"I'm sorry. I am just focused on this lesson. I want to know what you think about my routine. You have seen me play for several years, and know I have been working on my mental game. How consistent is it? Do you see any inconsistency with my routine?"

Alan thought for a moment before he replied and said, "You address the ball and get your feet settled at the same time you are taking your first look at the target. Then you look at the ball and take a waggle or two and settle down before taking a second look at the target. Next you look at the ball and take a swing, for the most part."

"For the most part? Does that mean I'm changing it up?" asked Kevin.

Alan replied, "Sometimes you take three looks. Why are you so concerned about this?"

Kevin reached in his bag and pulled out the last lesson. He opened the lesson and showed it to Alan. He had underlined a section from the lesson that read, *You can only think about one thing at a time.*

"According to what you just said, I don't have a defined Mental Program. How can I be aligning my feet and looking at the target at the same time? Shouldn't I get my club aligned to the target first and then focus on getting my feet and shoulders aligned?" asked Kevin.

Alan had a curious look on his face and replied, "I see

what you are saying, and I would have to agree. I just never thought about it. According to this letter, if you are consistent with your thought process, you will be consistent with your routine. This increases the consistency of your play. This sounds great!"

Over the next two hours, Alan and Kevin spent time organizing the steps to the Point of Alignment. They went through each step and made sure there was a specific purpose to it. If it did not have a purpose, they dropped that step. By the time the two hours went by, Kevin had a routine that was consistent.

During that week, Kevin played with Alan by his side. Kevin rehearsed the Preload and Mental Program while Alan made notes on his progress. It was interesting that Kevin's routine was more consistent in putting versus ball striking. Alan noticed it on the fourth hole on Friday. He pointed out to Kevin that he always took two looks at his line in putting.

"How is it possible that your routine in putting is so much better than on ball striking?" asked Alan.

"Is it? I don't know. What's the difference?" replied Kevin.

"The difference is you place the putter behind the ball and look at the line, then you settle your feet and take your grip, followed by the second look. After the second look, you look at the ball and putt. You seem to be doing this 90% of the time. Ball striking is only 50% to 60% of the time." said Alan.

At that moment Kevin made it a priority to work on his routine. He was putting really well in practice, and if Alan's assessment was correct, Kevin could only get better by the next tournament.

Chapter 9

The Point of Focus

Kevin had been doing great with his mental game and was getting ready for a big tournament, less than ten days away. I questioned if a week was long enough to learn and master the final part of the Mental Program. The Point of Focus was the most revealing step for me and could be a game changer for Kevin. After reading the journal, I realized how much I did not know about his approach to the game.

It was during this part of the process my thoughts were the most inconsistent. I often fell into the trap James mentioned in the beginning of the journal. If I had a negative thought, it would happen right before the shot. I would have thoughts like, "Don't hit it in the water. Don't run this putt by the hole. Please be good. I need this." These thoughts caused me to be all over the place mentally. As a result, my game was not consistent. I never looked at golf the way James did. The following is how James explained the Point of Focus.

Journal Entry

The final step in the Mental Program is the

Point of Focus. I found I needed to be focused right before I hit the shot. Many times a player will get quick with his swing and miss the shot. This is something that happened to me in my college years. I would run my routine until it was time to hit the shot, and that's when my thoughts would change. Sometimes I would have this passing thought, "Don't miss it right," or "You need this." These thoughts would kill my chances of executing a great shot.

I struggled to find a way to control my thoughts before takeaway. I needed a step to stay focused. I came up with the idea to have a specific thought I could duplicate on every shot. I wanted to have mental consistency throughout the process. The one thing I couldn't figure out was how to make this thought consistent. That all changed after my friend Johnny and I went clay shooting.

Johnny was in my history class during my sophomore year in college. He was always talking about shooting shotguns. I never shot a gun in my life. He would tell me how sporting clays was like golf. In fact, he would say it was golf with a shotgun. I didn't have a clue what he was talking about until one Saturday afternoon when he took me shooting.

I quickly found out why he called sporting clays golf with a shotgun. A golf course has 18 holes; this particular sporting clays course had 15 stations. Each station has a pair of targets the shooter would shoot at four times. Every station had a different pair. Sometimes the targets would cross each other in front of you, one going

The Point of Focus

left to right and the other right to left. Sometimes one would be going away from you and the other would be a looping target. There was even a target that rolled across the ground in front of you called a rabbit. It was hard for me to hit the clay target rolling and bouncing on the ground.

I had a great time shooting that day. Johnny was really good at explaining what I needed to do. What was even more thrilling was what I learned from that experience. In the beginning, I couldn't hit anything. I was really focused on the trap and wanted to make sure that I focused on the target when it came out of the trap.

Johnny laughed at me and said, "You can't hit what you can't see, James! You must look in front of the trap with a soft focus. Your eyes will follow the movement of the target. You will always miss the target if you focus on the trap. Setting the eyes with a soft focus in front of the trap allows you the ability to lock onto the clay target quickly." He was right. I started to hit some targets after making that change. Would this work in golf? Would it help me in my Mental Program?

I discovered when I set my eyes on the ball for a full second, my head position and eyes stayed down. When I was lazy with this eye set, my eyes would follow the club head during the takeaway. This was when I had the most inconsistent shots. It made sense. When I was shooting with Johnny and I was focusing on the trap, my eyes were locked on the trap and I couldn't follow the clay target. This is bad for shooting, but it's perfect for golf. When I focused on the ball, my eyes couldn't follow the club head.

All I needed now was to implement a thought that would occupy my Conscious Mind. How was I going to do this? I often struggled with thinking about the result. If there was danger to the right, and I was hitting the ball right that day, I would think "don't hit it to the right." Of course, I would hit the ball to the right and get a bad result. I kept thinking about my experience shooting sporting clays. Right before I called pull for the target, Johnny told me to think of something that gave me confidence. I would think "smooth" before I called pull. When I'm smooth, my performance is usually good.

What happened next amazed me! I would think smooth right before saying "pull." When I did this, I was really good at locking on the clay target and hitting it. I didn't think about hitting the target, I just did it. I couldn't believe it. Why was this so easy? Johnny explained that when you take the anticipation of hitting the target away, you improve the probability of hitting the shot. "It happens automatically," said Johnny. It made sense. If I'm thinking about hitting the target, I am consciously trying to hit the target, but when I think smooth it allows my subconscious to take over during the execution of the shot.

If you control your mind, you can improve the outcome. The Point of Focus allows this to happen. A player must focus on the ball and have a thought that allows him to hit the shot subconsciously. As I stated earlier, I came up with a criteria to find the appropriate thought.

The Point of Focus

First, the player must occupy the Conscious Mind. If you don't occupy your Conscious Mind, you will be doomed to a bad performance. The reason is the Conscious Mind wants to perform the task at hand. You must perform the task subconsciously in order to get the best result possible. This can only happen when you occupy the Conscious Mind. The goal is to park the Conscious Mind and let the subconscious take over.

Second, you must transfer power to the subconscious. This means that you must allow the shot to happen and not try to make it happen. Often, we try to make the shot happen the way we think it should. What we should do is let the shot happen and trust what we programmed in the Preload. I found when I doubted the shot I was about to hit, the result was poor. This part of the criteria puts the focus on trusting, and not trying. Trying is not the thing you want to do before hitting the shot.

I remember a conversation I had with my college coach. He said that there is no trying, only doing. He once asked me, "Do you want the pilot to try to land the plane?" I said, "No!" He replied, "Of course not, you want him to land the plane. You should have the same confidence in your golf game as he does in landing the plane." For me it was a turning point in understanding what commitment and confidence is all about.

The result of the shot shouldn't matter. What should matter is that I trust my decision and run a consistent thought process. This thought process allows me to let the shot happen. I don't care what the result is, only care about letting the shot happen and trusting the result will be good.

Third, you must keep it simple. Golf is already complicated. Why make it more complicated by having a confusing thought process before you hit the shot? This wasn't something that needed to be complex or complicated, but rather simple and easy to repeat.

Fourth, you must be able to duplicate the thought process. This means it doesn't matter what the shot is or what target you select. You should run the same thought process on an approach shot as you would with a driver on the tee box. Your Point of Focus is the same regardless of the shot and club selection.

Finally, the thought must be player specific. If the player doesn't have an emotional attachment to the Point of Focus, he won't be able to perform the Mental Program with the same level of effort each time. This makes this last part difficult. I used the same thought I used when shooting sporting clays with Johnny. I just thought smooth. By setting my eyes on the ball and thinking smooth, I couldn't think about anything else. This eliminated any negative thoughts that would enter my mind before the shot.

This part of the Mental Program was a true game changer for me. I never became a victim of my environment after this. I focused on only the thought process I had chosen in advance. This gave me an advantage over my competitors. They were focusing on what the environment was giving them to think about, and I was controlling my thoughts. With this mental approach, I now had an

The Point of Focus

advantage in tournaments.

This was eye opening for me. I could not believe what James had written. Why did I not think of this? I went my whole career being result-sensitive. I always changed my thoughts right before I hit the shot. I could not help it. If I had a chance to make an easy birdie, I would think about getting a shot back. James is saying something different. This could really change the way Kevin plays the game.

If Kevin takes the Point of Focus as seriously as the rest of the Mental Program, there is no doubt that he will reach a whole different level in his game. I could not wait to see how Kevin would do after learning the last part of the Mental Program.

To Kevin,

It is time for you to implement the last part of the Mental Program, the Point of Focus. This is the most important part of the Mental Program. The last thing a player needs to have happen is for a passing thought to interrupt his concentration. The Point of Focus helps with this. After you master this part of the Mental Program, you will have mental consistency like never before.

The Point of Focus has two parts. First, you must set your eyes on the ball for one to three seconds. This eye set is critical because without setting your eyes on the ball, your eyes will shift to the movement of the club head during the takeaway in the swing. When this happens, it affects the swing, and the results are not good. This is an unnecessary error that shouldn't happen. It doesn't matter where you focus the eyes. You can focus on a specific spot on the ball or have a general focus on the ball. It doesn't matter. What matters is that the eyes are set.

Second, you must have a thought that will hold your focus and promote a subconscious swing. This thought doesn't have to be related to golf. It can be anything, as long as it does the following. First, it must occupy your Conscious Mind. This means if you are thinking about somethin you have previously chosen and practiced, you can't think about anything else. Second, it must transfer power to the Subconscious Mind. This means you want to have the feeling of letting the shot happen and not making it happen. Third, keep this thought simple: the simpler, the better. Fourth, it must be duplicable. This means you can repeat the thought on every swing: a driver off the tee or an approach shot with a nine iron. And lastly, it must be player specific. The thought must be specific to you. You want a thought that is something you come up with that gives you confidence and allows the swing to happen.

The Point of Focus will allow you to have mental consistency before the action takes place. This will allow you to hit more consistent shots on a regular basis. This part of the Mental Program is designed to occupy the Conscious Mind and let the Subconscious Mind take over during the swing. There should be no thoughts during the swing. When you master this, along with the other parts of the Mental Program, you will see your scores come down and be more consistent.

Your Mentor

After finishing the lesson for Kevin, I had a feeling this was going to help him in a big way. It is hard to be mentally consistent, especially before hitting the shot. If a player could define the optimal thing to think about, that would provide him the best chance of getting a good result. Why would he think about anything else? He would not! This was the most important thing I had learned during this journey. Kevin was going to love this.

Chapter 10

The Invitational

When I arrived at the club early Tuesday morning to put the next lesson in Kevin's bag, he was already there. He was walking away from me headed to the driving range, golf bag over his shoulder, when I was walking up to the side door of the club. The thought crossed my mind, "How do I get this lesson to him?" He had his clubs and was headed to the driving range. I had to come up with some way to distract him.

I could not let Kevin know I was there. He thought I was out of town this week and I was meeting up with him next week at the Invitational. I took out my cell phone and called the pro shop, hoping that someone would answer the phone. No answer, of course. Now what would I do? I went around the side of the clubhouse to see where Kevin was. He was about half way to the driving range. My mind started racing with ways to distract him. I could not come up with anything, and then I heard something.

"What's up mate?"

I could not believe it! It was Paul, the Aussie boy of the club. Paul was the assistant pro and in charge that day. I smiled at him and with a joking tone said, "Why is Kevin walking to the driving range? Don't you provide him with a cart?"

His response was quick. "That joker won't wait for anything. I told him I was on my way and to give me five minutes. I'll go get him, bring him back up, and get him a cart. I'll catch up with you in a minute."

I told Paul I would see him when he got back. Now I had only two things to worry about. First, I had to get to Kevin's bag without him seeing me. Second, I hope Paul did not tell Kevin that he saw me.

There was a hillside that blocked the view of the driving range from the putting green. As I made my way down to the driving range, Paul was picking up Kevin on the far left side. Kevin had just started warming up when Paul pulled up to get him.

"Hey mate, why didn't you wait for me? Jump in and let me take you up to the clubhouse to get a cart for you," Paul said in a joking manner.

Kevin smiled and got into the cart with Paul. Once he was out of sight, I made a mad dash to his bag and put the lesson in the side pocket. I left like a bat out of hell, hoping no one saw me.

Throughout the week, Kevin kept making progress with his Mental Program. He started to put everything together, from the Point of Initiation to the Point of Focus. He was very consistent with the Point of Initiation. He was not rushing into the shot. He looked fluid and in control as he stepped into the shot. The Point of Alignment phase was done with the same rhythm and tempo, and he looked comfortable over the ball.

The progress in the final stage of the Mental Program was the most interesting part of the week. Kevin had an issue of rushing the shot after the confirmation look. Setting the eyes had been a challenge for him. Kevin would get impatient and it hurt his performance. If he could get the final step down, he could really make a giant step toward unlocking his true potential.

During the week, Kevin and Alan worked together to prepare for the Invitational. The Invitational is a tournament Kevin has struggled with in the past. The course has gotten the best of him over the years. Alan kept telling Kevin this tournament is all about running the Mental Program.

Alan came up with a brilliant idea. He had Kevin perform his Mental Program on the driving range, alternating shots at different targets. Alan videoed his shots and then sat down with Kevin to review his consistency. The results were obvious. Kevin had performed the Mental Program well until the final step. Some of the shots were quick, while other shots were performed perfectly.

When Alan played back the video, he timed the Mental Program of each shot. It became apparent that when Kevin was performing his Mental Program between thirteen to fourteen seconds, his results were better. This shows there is a direct correlation to running the Mental Program and the performance of the shot. The trick now was for Kevin to perform this on a consistent basis in tournaments.

My wife and I were excited to see Kevin compete this week. We caught up with him for lunch on Tuesday. He was in a very good mood. This was the most confident Kevin had been all year. He had a look in his eye that gave you the impression something good was going to happen. He told us how things had been going the past few weeks.

"You know about these lessons I have been receiving?" asked Kevin.

"Yes, what about them?" I replied.

"Well, I think I have a mental system now! I mean I have been playing this past week with ease. I feel I can trust my game. It's been a long time since I had this feeling going into a tournament," said Kevin.

"What has been the biggest difference for you?" I asked.

"The whole process-minded thinking has really helped. I think I was becoming too mechanical with my swing and way too result-oriented. This Preload and Mental Program has provided me with order and structure that I never had. If I can have the same experience in the tournament as in training, I can only imagine how good the performance will be," Kevin said.

Kevin did most of the talking during lunch. I smiled and was very interested in what he was saying. The week was going to be an event to remember. My wife and I talked a lot about Kevin that day. We both had seen him grow, and we were really excited to see him put all this together. This week was about opportunity. Kevin had the opportunity to put together a game plan that was totally different from any game plan in the past. For the first time in his career, he was going to make the mental game a priority.

I was nervous the first day. I could not help it. I just wanted to see Kevin put all these lessons in place. When I saw Kevin on the putting green, he was as cool as a cucumber. He showed no signs of being nervous. I asked Alan how his warm-up went.

"He hit the ball great and finished his warm-up running his Mental Program on various types of shots. He looks good. I have never seen him look so calm," said Alan.

My wife nudged me and said, "Let's go to the first green." She never likes to see Kevin hit his first shot. I don't know why. She always had this thing about being on the first green and watching Kevin from there.

As we walked to the green, we talked about watching the first tournament in Kevin's career as a pro. The difference in

The Invitational

that tournament and the way he handled himself today was striking. James would have been impressed at the growth in Kevin. The whole day was great. We saw Kevin play great golf and enjoyed the day together.

Kevin finished the round with a good performance. He was three under and only two shots back from the leader. He played a solid round. There were few mistakes in his game, and when he had poor shots, he bounced back quickly. On the fourth hole, he had a 15 footer to save par. He ran his program with precision and made the putt. It appeared easy for him. He kept putting himself in good situations and had opportunities to make birdies. Although he did not take advantage on every opportunity, he kept his composure throughout the round.

In the past, Kevin would have shown emotion after missing a good birdie opportunity. Today was different. He was solid throughout the round. He played well and his attitude after the round could not have been better. This was clear with his first comment outside the scoring tent.

"Did you see that? I played my game out there. Alan and I said we were only going to focus on the process, and it felt great. I feel like I could play another round of golf," said Kevin.

Kevin would have never made this comment in the past. It looked like all of his hard work was going to pay off this week. And, after the first three rounds, it looked very promising for Kevin to get his first win on tour. He played very consistently and was ten under going into the final round.

Kevin could not be in a better position to win. He was in the second to last group. He was sitting in third place, one shot behind the leaders and two shots ahead of fourth place. All the pressure was on the final pairing. Kevin could focus on his game and let the result fall into place. His attitude that afternoon was the same as it had been the whole week. He looked really good and was playing a solid round until hole 13.

Call me superstitious if you want, but I had a bad feeling on the par three 13th hole. Kevin was playing mistake-free golf up to that point and was four under for the day. That part was good. The bad part was the electronic scoreboard on the right side of the green. While Kevin was getting ready to hit his tee shot, I noticed that scoreboard. Kevin was in first place with a one shot lead. The thought of him seeing that scoreboard and falling into his old habit of being result-focused stayed in my mind like a broken record.

Kevin reached in his back pocket and pulled out his yardage book. He took about 30 seconds to review it and looked at Alan and said, "You think 7 with a slight draw is the play?"

"Sounds good to me," replied Alan.

Kevin hit a good shot, but got a bad bounce. It landed on the downslope just past the front bunker and kicked left to the back of the green. This left him with a tricky, 30 foot plus birdie putt.

When Kevin approached the green, the crowd noise was loud. These fans were going crazy. The noise went on for a good three minutes.

After the crowd settled down a fan yelled, "You got this Kevin, take it home and win this thing!"

Until then Kevin was not aware of his position in the tournament. But now he knew. He looked up at the scoreboard and saw his name on the top of that leaderboard. A smile appeared on his face as he turned to Alan. As Alan cleaned Kevin's ball, he was smiling too. It was great to see them enjoying the moment, but the feeling I had would not go away. I just wanted him to continue to perform like he had all week.

When Kevin putted, he made an aggressive stroke and the ball rolled six feet past the cup. He looked solid in his program. On his next putt he was unlucky. Kevin had a left to right breaking putt that was slightly uphill. Just like the putt before he looked good during his Mental Program, but the ball just lipped out of the cup and settled on the left edge. He tapped in for bogey and was going into the 14th hole tied for first with two other players.

This makes the game so difficult. One hole you can be ahead, and the next hole you can be behind. The leaderboard is constantly changing, and this day was no exception. Kevin would play the remaining holes well, but his body language changed. He did not play with the same flow and rhythm he had on the first nine holes; nevertheless, he gave himself a chance to win. You cannot win if you do not put yourself in position to win. Finishing tied for third was not bad and it was not as painful to watch, but it was not the victory I was hoping for.

The difference with this tournament, compared to the others, was Kevin was not out of it. He played well enough to win, but at this level you have to finish strong. His game changed after he saw himself in the lead. He did not look like the same player after the bogey on the 13th hole. I could not wait to talk to him and get his view on how he felt about the tournament.

Kevin and Alan met us outside the players' locker room to talk about the round. Alan said, "What a ride that was!"

Kevin followed, "I feel disappointed in the way I finished. I thought things were going well and I just couldn't close the door at the end."

"When did you start thinking differently out there?" I asked.

"It was on the 13th green when I heard that guy yell out, 'Win this thing!' I looked up and saw my name on the top of the leaderboard, and all I could think about was to stay there.

I felt like I had to make a par, and when I didn't do that, I started to focus on the score," Kevin replied.

I asked, "Did that affect how you ran your Mental Program?"

"I guess so. What do you think, Alan?"

"It was obvious you weren't as consistent in your routine. I felt you did a better job from tee to green compared to how you ran your routine on putts, which is interesting because it was opposite of how things went in practice last week."

Kevin's response was interesting: "I don't know what to think. I felt like my mental game was solid until hole 13. How could I not think about the result when I knew I had a chance to win? The last thing I wanted to do was to let this one slip away. I have already done that this year."

"That's the key! You just made a great point. Once you started to focus on where you were and the fact that you could win this tournament, your thought process changed. When you changed from running your mental system to results thinking, your performance suffered. You need to make the mental game the priority throughout the tournament and not be concerned how you finish," I said.

"That sounds like I'm accepting defeat and not caring. I really want to win," Kevin replied.

Alan jumped in and said, "We are not asking that you change how much you care. We are talking about changing what you care about. What if you did that? What if you just focused on this mental system and made it the priority, not caring about the score or where you finish on the leaderboard? I think your uncle is onto something. Next week we should make that the game plan. I'll keep track of where you are, and you just focus on the process and let's just see what happens."

"You're right! I have always focused on winning and it hasn't helped me as a pro golfer. Maybe I should just focus on making the mental game the priority, and just accept whatever happens. Let's go with that plan next week. I just want to go out and have fun and not worry anymore," replied Kevin.

The plan was set for next week. I am excited because Kevin's wife and son would be at that event. I think he will focus more on process. Off to the next tournament we go.

Chapter 11

The Classic

We had dinner with Kevin and his family on Tuesday evening. We talked about how things were going with Sara, Kevin's wife, and Jimmy, his son. It was a great visit that evening. Sara shared photos of the trip she took with her mom and sister. Her sister also has a little boy who is one year older than Jimmy. They went to Florida together and took the two boys to Disney World. They had been planning a mother and sister trip for the past three years.

Sara was in a great mood that evening, and Jimmy was as active as ever. Jimmy is a quiet and shy four year old, but today was an exception. This time he could not stop talking about his experience at Disney World. He begged Sara to show more pictures of him with Goofy, the different rides and the places they visited. I had a grin on my face and was excited for him. Sara was all smiles. She must have had five hundred pictures on her iPhone, each one with a story behind it.

Golf never came up in the conversation. We focused on Sara and Jimmy and talked about the holidays that were coming up in a couple of months. My wife and I try to support and share the holiday experiences with Kevin and his family as much as possible. We see them for Thanksgiving or New Year's. One year Kevin will have Christmas at his house, and the next year they will go to Des Moines, Iowa to visit Sara's parents and Sara's sister's family.

My wife and I were excited to see how Kevin would do this week. He was very relaxed leading up to his tee time on Thursday morning at 8:50. As usual, we went to the first green to watch Kevin. The first hole had a great hole location. We stood on the right side of the green, next to the ropes, and we had a great view of the green. Kevin's approach shot looked like a bullet coming in our direction. It was an awesome shot that started out toward us and worked back to the left toward the hole. The shot almost landed in the cup, missing the hole by two inches when it landed, leaving an easy two-foot birdie putt. What a way to start the tournament.

Kevin was a machine. He birdied the first three holes and followed that up with two pars. As we walked up to the sixth green, Sara caught up with us. She had dropped Jimmy off at the day care center provided by the tour. She asked how Kevin was doing. I explained how he started off, and she smiled and replied, "I can't tell you how excited Kevin has been. I can say his attitude toward golf has really improved since receiving the letters. He has been more content and is more consistent with his play. The things he has taken from those letters have really made a positive impact on him. I'm sure he has shared that with you."

"Yes, he has. I have seen a real impact on his attitude and his commitment to the game. I feel this is going to help him win at this level."

Sara talked about Kevin's passion for the game. She went on about how his passion for perfecting the mental side of golf has rejuvenated him. "He is a different player now. He is a lot more calm and relaxed before tournaments, a lot more like he was in college."

As Sara continued to talk about Kevin's attitude and progress, Kevin went on to birdie the sixth hole and par the next three. He was playing with confidence and looked very relaxed. As we headed to the tenth tee box, Kevin looked over to us and smiled, giving a big thumbs up. Alan walked over to us and said in a quiet voice, "He's doing awesome and having fun."

This is the type of player I only saw in practice when we would play together. He is playing in the biggest tournament of the year like he had with me on the weekend at our home course. I wondered how long this would last. He had never looked so calm and cool in a tournament.

As the round continued, Kevin played very well. He birdied four more holes and only had one bogey, the tough par three 14th hole. It did not phase him. He played so well that he had a two shot lead going into day two. He made shooting a 65 look easy.

After the round we went to the scoring tent and waited to congratulate Kevin on a great performance. Normally we would just wait a few minutes while he signed his scorecard, but this time was different. This was the Classic, a big tournament. The media was waiting for him for an immediate interview. We waited for 30 minutes before he made his way to us.

We talked to Alan during Kevin's interviews. He could not stop smiling. "Did you see that performance?" Alan asked. "He didn't say anything about score today. He only asked about distance and talked about what shot was best to make. Between shots we talked about what movies to watch. Movies! We never have had that type of conversation during the round. It was incredible to see him run his Mental Program!"

Awesome was exactly how I would define his day. He played the way Kevin should play, which was having fun and making the most out of the game of golf. Too many times he would get ahead of himself and start thinking about how he was doing. Today was a perfect example of what James was talking about in the journal. It was all about the process and having fun. Let the score happen and only think about the things that are important, letting the other things go. Today Kevin did that.

The following morning was interesting. I did not sleep well. All I kept thinking about was how Kevin was going to follow up day one. It had been a long time since I had seen him play that well in a big tournament. His ability to play was not what worried me. It was his ability to stay focused that concerned me. I did not want him to have the same experience as last week.

I kept recalling a statement in James' journal: "You must make the mental game the priority. Focus on the process, not the outcome." Would Kevin be able to do that today? Making the mental game the priority is all about running the mental system and not concerning yourself with where you are in the tournament. He did not tee off until 1:30, and everyone had been congratulating him on a great day one performance.

My wife and I met Kevin and Alan near the putting green and wished them good luck. He had a smile of his face and did not say much. He just mentioned he felt great and he was ready to play. Alan was much more talkative.

"I feel like today will be the day to test Kevin. The weather is good and he is feeling great. I'm just hoping he will duplicate the same performance as yesterday, but I'm nervous about today. He isn't saying too much. I'm not sure if that is a good thing." said Alan.

As we made our way to the first green, my wife made an

interesting comment. "I feel this will be his worst day of the tournament for Kevin."

"How could you say something like that?" I replied.

"You, of all people, know about the pendulum affect. He played great yesterday. Today he will not play as well. A lot of times you follow a great performance with a bad one. Just like you often follow a bad performance with a good one. Don't you think that is weighing on his mind?" she asked.

"I hope not! I hope he's thinking the same as yesterday. I would like to see him run away with this tournament," I replied with a gasp.

"I do, as well, but you know that's not likely. I'm just saying today his performance will be the worst of the four days. I'm not saying he will play badly. I'm just not getting my hopes up. I really think he will do fine. I just don't think he can maintain what he did yesterday until he duplicates that performance," she said.

I shook my head and replied, "I can't believe you would be pessimistic about this. You played golf competitively. Weren't you optimistic about your play? I can't believe I'm hearing this from you."

Her reply was quick: "I'm not pessimistic. I'm a realist."

Realist or not, I changed the subject. We followed Kevin and watched every shot. I knew yesterday was a great performance for Kevin. I just believed all this focus on the mental game had put him in a better position to handle the pressure that came with the territory of being the leader.

As the day went on, I could only shake my head. Hole after hole, I waited to see him get a birdie streak going. That did not happen. Kevin started out par, par, birdie, par. He kept getting birdie opportunities, but he was not taking advantage of them.

It was a long afternoon and my stomach was turning the

whole time. Maybe my wife was right. Maybe I was getting ahead of things and thinking Kevin was going to win. Kevin had made a lot of progress, but he had not seen that breakthrough. The day was not a bad day for Kevin, however it was not a good day either. He managed to shoot even par, hardly the score you would expect after a 65.

That evening Kevin said something that really caught my attention. "I didn't play that well today, but I ran my Mental Program well. I felt like I duplicated my process from the first day. Today could have been a disaster. For the first time in my golf career, I feel good about a performance that didn't produce a low score. I know why my score wasn't better. In the past I would have focused on the outcome and not on the process. I had a good mental performance. I just need to make some adjustments technically."

Wow! What a change in Kevin's attitude! I could not believe how he analyzed his performance. I was the one that was looking at the result. He was not looking at the score, he was looking at his overall performance. This was going to make the weekend very interesting.

Kevin was in the final group on Saturday and was one shot behind leader of the tournament. This tournament kept getting more stressful. I did not know if I should be excited, or nervous, for him. I guess I should have been happy he was only one shot back, but I was on pins and needles at this point.

By the time Kevin teed off, the weather had made a turn. The week had been nice, and the wind was hardly a factor. That all changed. The winds picked up on the fourth hole. This made it more challenging for the players, but Kevin played like he was in another world. He played the course like a champion chess player controls the chess board.

Some of the shots Kevin executed were performed with near-perfection. On the ninth hole, with a brutal headwind,

The Classic

Kevin hit a low screaming driver into the wind. He outdrove his playing partner by 30 yards. It was incredible! He managed to reach the long par four in two and drained a ten foot birdie putt. It was amazing to watch him play in tough conditions. His opponent was frustrated and showed his emotions throughout the round, but Kevin was the opposite. Kevin was focused and calm. He put on a display of confidence I had not seen.

When Kevin walked up to the final hole, he had a commanding four shot lead. He played the type of golf he needed to play, smart and error-free. He was making good decisions, and the last hole was the most challenging on the course. The way the wind was blowing made this par five extremely tough. The dog leg left gave the players a strong crosswind on the second shot. This made for an interesting decision for the players. You could try to go for the green in two with a wood or try to lay up in a tight narrow fairway.

The choice was a tough one for the players to make today. If you were able to reach the green in two, you had a good chance to make birdie. If you failed to reach it in two, you were looking at a tough pin location with a strong left to right wind.

On the second shot, Kevin reached in his bag and pulled out a six iron. He was going to lay up at 100 yards, his go-to yardage. Kevin has always been deadly from 100 yards. He loved to play a low punch shot with his nine iron. It was a shot he had worked on his entire life, and with these winds it was the type of shot that would give him an advantage.

As Kevin took his practice swings, the wind began to pick up. It was now blowing left to right and into Kevin. He looked at Alan and said, "Get the five iron." He was making a change that was unusual for him. Kevin has never changed clubs after his practice swings, but this time it was the correct move. He hit a brilliant shot to the right side of the fairway that left him 105 yards from the pin. However, what was more amazing than the shot was the angle he had to the pin.

Kevin could not have placed the ball in a better location. He had a straight shot at the pin dead into the wind. Alan looked at Kevin and said, "You want to play that low punch shot, don't you?"

Kevin reached in the bag and pulled out his nine iron and said, "Watch this."

I do not know how he hit the shot, but it was the shot of the day. He took a three quarter swing and hit a low straight shot at the pin that landed three feet short and rolled up to one foot from the cup: the easiest birdie putt you could ask for. He was acting, and playing, like it was a routine day at the club. He was the only player to post a score under 70 that day. If he duplicated this tomorrow, no one would be able to catch him.

On the final day, Kevin asked me to meet him on the driving range. He wanted to show me something, and I was to eager to see what he had. As my wife and I walked up to the driving range, we could hardly keep from smiling. Both of us were excited for Kevin in this position. For some players, this was the toughest position to be in. He had a five shot lead and that lead could vanish if he did not play well.

Kevin walked over to the ropes, pulled out his scorecard cover and said, "Look at this." It was a note inside the scorecard cover that read "Process is Primary, run your system." Kevin looked me in the eye and said, "I could hardly sleep last night. All I could think about was what I need to shoot in order to win this thing. I can't think that way. I have played the past three days thinking about committing to the Preload and running the Mental Program. Alan and I came up with this idea over breakfast. What do you think?"

"I think it's brilliant!" I replied.

The Classic

"Every time I think of score or winning the tournament, I'm going to pull this out and read it. I think this is going to help me stay with the process and not get caught up in the tournament," Kevin said.

I felt really good about Kevin's approach to the round. He was focusing on his strategy and coming up with ways to stick with his plan. This day would be the day that would define him as a player. It was time to see if he had what it takes to win at this level.

As you might think, Kevin started out shaky. He was one over after five holes, and things began to look questionable. His lead went from five shots to two. Brian Benders, the leading money earner on tour, was closing in on Kevin. Brian had already won twice this year and had proven to be a threat in this position.

On the tee box on hole six, Kevin pulled out his scorecard cover and opened it. He read his note and took a deep breath. What happened next surprised me. He looked at Alan, smiled, and said, "I'm ready to play now." I guess he was right, because he birdied the next three holes.

Kevin was making the turn at two under par with a four shot lead. As he walked up to the tee box, he kept his note in his left hand and read it again. I thought he was playing well and looked in control. Why would he need to read the note again?

The next three holes were solid par holes. With six holes left, Kevin was in a great position. If he parred out, he would win the tournament, but if he faltered he could lose the tournament. On the 12th green, Kevin had a seven-foot putt to save par. It was fairly straight with a little right to left break. As he approached the putt, Kevin took a deep breath. He looked at his spot and made three practice strokes. As Kevin lined up the putter and set his feet, a roar from the eighteenth green erupted. Brian Benders eagled the par five 18th hole and was now one shot behind Kevin.

Kevin did not back off his putt. He took an extra look at the spot and made his stroke. It was his first crucial mistake. Kevin should have backed off, but he did not. He missed the putt and took a bogey. Now with six holes left, Kevin needed to finish strong to win the tournament.

The next three holes were solid pars and Kevin was looking like he did earlier. He walked up to the 16th tee with a grin on his face. He performed his Mental Program perfectly and hit the longest drive of the day. He was now 140 yards out. He would stick his approach shot within six feet for a birdie opportunity and put himself in position to regain the lead. As Kevin lined up his birdie putt a fan yelled, "Put it in the HOLE!" Kevin paused, stepped back, and took two more practice strokes. He then ran his program and drained the birdie putt. When he handed his putter to Alan, he said, "I didn't hear a thing, did you?"

As Alan smiled from ear to ear, Kevin grinned and made his way to the 17th tee. He was like a machine from that point on. He made the last two holes look easy. He finished strong with three birdies and won the tournament by three strokes. When things started to look like they were going to take a turn for the worse, he turned things around. What an amazing day!

Kevin finally had his breakthrough. I saw a different player. He was in control; he knew what he had to do, and he did it. After the round was over, we all congratulated him. He looked at me and said, "I'm taking next week off to celebrate. This has been a long time coming."

I invited Kevin and Sara over to celebrate his victory that following weekend. We grilled out, sat outside on the patio and talked about his victory. Kevin was all smiles and when the moment presented itself, I asked Kevin the following

The Classic

question: "Do you know who you can thank for your success?"

Kevin's response was immediate, "Absolutely, it's the person who left me those letters. Those lessons made a huge impact on how I view my game. I have made progress because now I understand what was missing. These lessons have made a huge impact on my progression as a player."

"Wait a minute! It was you who put those lessons in my bag, right?"

I looked at him with a smile and nodded my head. I realized I had made a significant difference in his life. For a brief moment, I knew what it must feel like to be a father.

Troy Bassham is a Senior Master Instructor and Director of Systems Development at Mental Management® Systems LLC. Troy has been teaching Mental Management® since 1995. His main focus is helping players develop mental consistency during play, performing under pressure, building the Self-Image of a winner, and adopting training principles that focus on developing the mind and body at the same time. Troy's clients have won local, state, national and world events using Mental Management®. Troy has worked with hundreds of junior athletes with their mental game developing dozens of National Champions.

Troy used Mental Management® himself to win 12 National Championships in international rifle shooting, setting four National Records, and winning the CISM World Championship.

Troy provides one-on-one, small group and large group training options.

Contact Troy at:

Mental Management® Systems LLC
700 Parker Square
Suite 140
Flower Mound, TX 75028
ph. 972-899-9640
info@mentalmanagement.com
www.mentalmanagement.com

Attainment by Troy Bassham

Learn the 12 Elements of Elite Performance What separates the best from the rest! Troy talks about the 3 step training rule, becoming mentally strong, Self-Image, opportunity, passion, participation levels, and much more! A great addition to your mental training library for any competition, performer or business professional! *Attainment* is available as a soft cover book, 2 CD set, or as a download.

Order today at:
www.mentalmanagementstore.com

Notes